CONTENTS

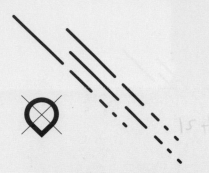

INTRODUCTION

Soldiers of the BTS ARMY, welcome to the ultimate BTS fan book, your access-all-areas sneak-peek behind the scenes, and beyond the stars, with the planet's biggest pop group and your new favourite band... BTS!

For the first time in music history, an Asian band is lighting up the whole world with their illuminating messages of love and understanding through self-penned and produced songs that cover an eclectic mix of genres – from hip-hop to rap-pop, super-charged EDM to breathtaking power ballads. We are, of course, talking about the world's one and only K-pop phenomenon septet – BTS!

As a mega-fan, you'll know that BTS don't do things by halves – they do things by threes! The seven-piece group have, since their inception in 2013, released (rather prolifically) a string of record-breaking, award-winning and bestselling EPs, albums and tour trilogies, as well as – how could we forget! – reality TV and internet shows. There is also their fantastic Bangtan Bomb YouTube series, which features clips of their chaotic daily lives and tours, and showcases each one of the group's members' distinct personality and style. And what super style and personality they all have! (Especially Jimin – just kidding.)

From oldest to youngest, the band's seven "hella lit" members are Jin, Suga, J-Hope, Rap Monster or RM, Jimin, V and Jungkook. Each member adds their own separate, but complementary, style and flavour to the band's sonic and stylish chemistry, allowing BTS to flourish as a one-of-a-kind seven-piece never seen before in western music charts and the beaming beacon of the reinvented

K-pop (or K-hip-hop) movement currently conquering the world. Leading the charge is BTS. And there is no band better than BTS.

But BTS are more than just performers of their infectious pop-rap, razor-sharp dance choreography for their huge social-media following – BTS say and do more than their contemporaries for, and on behalf of, all the social injustices in the world. As always, RM says it best. He is the band's main English spokesperson, and as he told *Time* magazine in 2017: "We came together with a common dream to write, dance and produce music that reflects our musical backgrounds as well as our life values of acceptance, vulnerability and being successful." He concluded: "Music transcends language."

BTS get out of bed every day for their ARMY (standing for "Adorable Representatives of MC for Youth") of devoted fans, fans who have turned BTS into the first K-pop band to break the Top 30 on the US Billboard Hot 100 (with their track "MIC Drop", remixed by US DJ Steve Aoki) and made the group become the most tweeted-about set of artists in 2017. Even esteemed American talk-show host, Ellen DeGeneres (who welcomed the group to her show in 2017) likened the band's reception to American shores to that of Beatlemania in the 1960s. Not an unsurprising comparison, really: after all, you can't spell "Beatles" without "BTS"!

On Twitter, BTS is the first South Korean group to achieve 10 million followers. They are the first K-pop group to perform at the American Music Awards and the first South Korean group to win a Billboard Music Award. That all happened in one year! That's a huge achievement, and an event that will open the gates for many more Asian artists to break down barriers and begin seeing their music make waves in the western musical landscape. But this is all just the beginning for BTS. They have so much more of the world to conquer. With their first massive world tour that started in August 2018, BTS are on a path to sweep the world off its feet with their music and personally thank each and every one of their fans in their home cities. That's why BTS are so awesome – they emotionally resonate with their army of fans in a way that feels sincere... because it is authentic. The boys mean everything they say and do.

BTS may hail from South Korea – probably the only group in your download collection that does! – but now they belong to the world. They're the right band at the right time.

But how much do you know about these Korean idols? Let's find out!

Over to you, boys...

> "A LOT OF PEOPLE SAY THIS, BUT IT'S REALLY TRUE FOR US: WE ARE LIVING A DREAM, ALL SEVEN OF US, BEING ABLE TO PURSUE WHAT WE LOVE. WE STRIVE TO PUT EVERYTHING INTO OUR MUSIC. OUR LYRICS DEAL WITH REAL ISSUES THAT FACE ALL HUMANS: CHOICES IN LIFE, DEPRESSION, SELF-ESTEEM. AND THE FANS KNOW THAT WE ARE THERE FOR THEM, AND THEY ARE THERE FOR US."
> RM

LEFT The boys rock the mic at their debut showcase, Ilchi Art Hall, Seoul, June 15, 2013.

BEFORE THE STARDOM

Bangtan Sonyeondan (Bulletproof Boy Scouts), Beyond the Scene, or even The Bangtan Boys – take your pick! – BTS have several of the most interesting boy-band names you will have heard in recent years. But that's because they are the most refreshing boy band you've heard in recent years too – a fascinating result of the way in which they all first met, coming together from very distinct regions of South Korea, and uniting all of their inspirations together to form something the world had never seen or heard before...

BEFORE THE BIG BANG

When the seven members of the band first came together – through individual auditions at Big Hit Entertainment in Seoul, South Korea, between 2010 and 2013 – BTS, and their mentor, CEO of Big Hit Entertainment, Bang Si-hyuk, wanted the group to mean something more than just music. Bang had a vision. He yearned for the group to "become a band that defies prejudices and discriminations against the young generation." All seven members, plus Bang, including first member RM, sought out a South Korean group that did more than just perform "bubblegum pop" with no explanation or reason. The pair wanted a group with a mission. A band with something to say. They wanted them to be "well-balanced between message and performance" and to "adapt the trendiest pop genres so that anyone can enjoy regardless of cultural and language barriers", and emit a unified sound created by the "special chemistry made by seven personalities in the band." This mission was to be shared by all seven members. "I don't want anyone in the band who wants to become a celebrity," said Bang of his "trainee" selection process of the members, as the concept of BTS was shaping in 2010. "I don't want to work with anyone whose goal is to be an entertainer and wants to try to use songs as a means to do so. You have to love the music as much as the stage. My philosophy and worldview is instilled in BTS. BTS are kids who do music relentlessly."

BROTHERS IN ARMS

Choosing and selecting the correct members for his trainee programme was a careful and considered round of auditions of talented musicians from all over South Korea. The process took two years. "From the beginning I wanted people who knew what they wanted to do, and consequently we found people like that, so I'm happy," commented Bang. "BTS don't just move according to whatever's planned. They create their own music, they manage their schedule. If they can't do that, the next album won't come out. What they want to wear is also clear." For those critics thinking that BTS are just another boy band, think again.

"All BTS members had self-motivation from their early teenage years," Bang made clear in a 2013 interview. "Before joining Big Hit, they all struggled despite exceptional enthusiasm in their respective areas of music and dance." The group's individual struggle to get their voices heard would come to unite Jin, Jimin, V, Jungkook, RM, Suga and J-Hope and is what fuelled them all to audition for Big Hit Entertainment to begin with. They wanted to be found.

Rap Monster was the first to audition for Bang. He passed with flying colours. Naturally.

"Back in 2010, I was introduced to Bang Si-hyuk, our executive producer and CEO of Big Hit Entertainment," recalled RM, the only truly fluent English speaker in BTS, and hence the main representative for them in interviews. "I was an underground rapper and only 16 years old, a freshman at high school. Bang thought I had potential as a rapper and lyricist."

"The first opportunity to plan BTS was leader Rap Monster," verified Bang. "RM is extremely self-reflective, sophisticated and philosophical, considering his age. After seeing his rap [at his audition] I thought about creating a hip-hop group and gathered the

OPPOSITE ABOVE The boys arrive in style at their first award show – the 2013 Melon Music Awards, Olympic Gymnastics Stadium, Seoul, November 14, 2013.

OPPOSITE BELOW Performing in sync at one of their earliest live performances as a septet, Hallyu Dream Concert, Gyeongju, October 5, 2013.

current members. Later, I thought that the group shouldn't just be idols who do hip-hop, but rather members who can tell their own stories. This thought has consistently been reflected in BTS's music and has not changed now. I wanted the group to not only compose and write lyrics but also independently participate in producing and stage management."

It was Bang's vision that every member of the band be as vital as the next and that the chemistry between them all should unite them to become a meaningful unit. Without this key element, BTS would just be the same as every other K-pop boy band that never found success outside of their home nation. The reason the band release albums and tour as trilogies is because of Bang's concept that each member should "tell a story" and that it was "not possible to put all of the stories BTS wanted to tell on one album", hence the prolific output of music in a format that would be considered unthinkable by any other band, and is, indeed, quite alien to western ears.

TRAINEES BECOME IDOLS
Over the course of two years, Big Hit Entertainment held auditions for the other members. "Suga joined, then J-hope, who was really popular as a dancer in his hometown. We were the first three!" remembered RM.

The members are often cited as coming exclusively from Seoul, the capital city of South Korea, but in fact, the band's members hail from many distant regions of their country, showcasing the fact that Bang really did look far and wide to find the perfect ingredients for his BTS masterpiece. RM is from Ilsan, Jin is from Gwacheon, J-Hope is from Gwangju, Jimin and Jungkook are from Busan, and Suga and V are from Daegu. The group grew up far apart, but their desire to be part of something bigger brought them together.

"We started as a hip-hop crew, and Bang felt that there should be singers that talk about things needed by the society," said RM of their humble hip-hop beginning. "We were rappers who could actually realize his idea, and we had members with performance skills. The more important thing is that our music and performance must have a superior quality because, before anything, we are singers. We had that ability, and our sincerity, messages, and communication were all added in, and Bang fully supported us. He gave us freedom to become players, and we, as players, could take high risk to get high return. Big Hit and the band equally contributed, and I think this is a desirable business model where agency and artist collaborate as business partners."

In 2014, as the band prepared to release *2 Cool 4 Skool*, they were living together (they still do!) in a cramped house and sleeping in one room (they now have their own rooms!). The seven different artists, talented in their own right across the whole spectrum of creative arts – acting, dancing, rapping, singing, choreography, performance – and brought together from all over their country, knew that in order to be successful they had to be authentic. And being authentic meant they had to be more than just newfound friends. "The seven of us have pushed each other to be the best we can be," revealed RM. "It has made us as close as brothers."

ABOVE Lighting up the MBC Music 'Show Champion', Uniqlo AX-Hall, Seoul, October 9, 2013.

OPPOSITE The band show off their bling at 2013's Incheon Korean Music Wave photo call, September 1, 2013.

"IF YOU TEACH A K-POP ARTIST ENGLISH AND SIGN WITH AN AMERICAN COMPANY, THAT IS JUST BASICALLY ASIANS DEBUTING IN THE AMERICAN MARKET. THAT IS NOT K-POP."
BANG SI-HYUK

HITMAN BANG

"I made a promise with BTS before they debuted," said Bang Si-hyuk, AKA Hitman Bang, often regarded as South Korea's answer to Simon Cowell, the creator and fair but often harsh judge on worldwide TV smashes *American Idol*, *Britain's Got Talent* and *The X Factor*. "I promised that I would help them become an established team as a producer if they believed in the team's potential and do their best with their individual responsibilities. The members believed in my promise and I also did my best to honour my words."

It is Bang who can take the credit for the initial success and selection of each member of BTS. While their success since has been down to their chemistry and songwriting, it was Bang who engineered these particular seven individuals to come together in the first place. Bang saw something in each member – a quality that he knew would bond with the band mates. Bang founded Big Hit Entertainment in 2005 after a few years of songwriting hits for the "first generation" of K-pop bands, including g.o.d and Rain (a vital influence on many of the band members).

"The first reason people love BTS is because their music is based on my love for hip-hop music," claimed Bang in an interview. But it wasn't just hip-hop that made BTS stand out, it was their individual desires to sing songs that spoke to their fans. "Whereas most K-pop songs deal with love or break-up, BTS's music deals with ideas involving school and youth and expresses contemporary stories that everyone can relate to," revealed Bang. "I think many people like them because they don't just have commonplace love songs. BTS has a unique voice that unravels worries experienced through growth and the uneasiness of youth. Also, in the context of their music being relatable, the members show a friendly charm. I think another reason is their desire to communicate with their fans."

KIM SEOK-JIN

Mr Worldwide Handsome, Kim Seok-jin, or just Jin, to his band mates, is the oldest member of BTS. Born on December 4, 1992, Jin is one of BTS's four principal vocalists as showcased on the rather incredible *Wings* solo track "Awake". Jin was discovered on the streets of Seoul and is now as famous for his love of food as he is for his incredible singing voice, as anyone who watches his delectable Eat Jin internet TV show will know.

"PERFORMING IN A CONCERT WAS MY DREAM. I WANTED TO BECOME ONE TOGETHER WITH OUR FANS THROUGH OUR MUSIC." JIN

ACTOR WITH THE X FACTOR

Before BTS fame and superstardom found Jin, through his auditions for Big Hit Entertainment in 2012, he was studying film at Konkuk University, Seoul. Born and raised in Anyang City in the Gyeonggi-do province, before moving to Gwacheon city, Jin believed that he would follow in his family's footsteps and work with nature, as a farmer. It was unthinkable to him that he would be given the opportunity to become a global singing superstar.

As a child, Jin hated to stand still – he was always on the move and disliked his school studies. "I was a vigorous child in elementary school," he has said. "My favourite subject at school was Physical Education. It's the exact opposite to now!"

At high school, Jin believed he may start a career as a journalist, but that faded away when his love of acting started to blossom and his deep passion for film developed. "The dream of becoming an actor was born in my second year of high school, after watching Kim Nam Gil-ssi in the drama *Queen Seondeok*," he has revealed. "I was touched and thought that I wanted to make people cry with my acting too. So I studied Film at Konkuk university."

It was while studying in Seoul that Jin was spotted on the streets by Bang Hit Entertainment. He was seen getting off a bus by a Big Hit Entertainment representative who thought Jin had just the style and look the agency was looking for to fill their new seven-piece band, being put together by Bang Si-hyuk. Jin was invited to audition. He won a spot in the band, despite having no experience of singing or dancing! Jin was the oldest member to audition. "Three months after starting film school, I was scouted by Big Hit and became a trainee. Jungkook joined two days after me," remembers Jin, speaking of the group's youngest member, who was only 15 at the time.

While Jin enoyed his life as a Big Hit trainee – a process that Bang Si-hyuk installed to ensure all members of BTS could fulfill their duties as part of the band – Jin began his life in BTS under-confident of his performing and songwriting abilities. He was certain he couldn't dance or write songs, but thanks to his BTS brothers and band mates, Jin soon found the confidence to express himself and his artistic talents. "My interest in music started after I met the members," Jin recalled. "Back in the earliest days, I couldn't even think I can write songs. Thanks to the influence from our members, I'm now continuing to write songs. Even though they aren't at the level of being put into albums yet, I get good responses."

One day, Jin hopes he can funnel all of his energy into acting in a film – but for now, his love of music and performing, and being with his best friends on stage, comes first. That and telling Dad jokes – much to the annoyance of his BTS band mates!

OPPOSITE Jin rocks a suave and sophisticated look at the Gaon Chart K-Pop Awards, February 17, 2016.

LEFT Mr Worldwide Handsome in action!

HIT RECORD

2 COOL 4 SKOOL

While fans know that BTS became a big hit with the success of their 2016 album *Wings*, and the huge 2015 single "I NEED U", it was with their debut album, the seven-track *2 Cool 4 Skool* that BTS broke through the barriers and popped the K-pop balloon with a powerful pop-influenced bang.

TRACKLISTING:
Intro: 2 Cool 4 Skool
(feat. DJ Friz)
We Are Bulletproof Pt.2
Skit: Circle Room Talk
No More Dream
Interlude
I Like It
Outro: Circle Room Cypher
Skit: On the Start Line
(Hidden Track)
Path (Hidden Track)

ABOVE Onstage at the Incheon K-Pop Concert, September 21, 2014.

RIGHT Causing red carpet chaos at the Gaon Chart K-Pop Awards, Olympic Park, Seoul, January 28, 2015.

The beginning of BTS's career as a rap-pop phenomenon began with their "Skool" trilogy of albums, beginning with their debut record 2 Cool 4 Skool, followed by 2013's O!RUL8,2? and Skool Luv Affair EPs. This Skool trilogy features lyrics and tracks that relate to the everyday lives, themes and relationships of teenage students at school. While their 2015–16 trilogy EP, The Most Beautiful Moment in Life (Part 1, 2 and Epilogue) saw the band "grow up" and experiment with more young-adult lyrical themes and high-energy dance sonics, it was the Skool trilogy that perfectly laid the foundation of the BTS vision of being a band that carefully thought about how their lyrics could deeply resonate with their fans, all of whom they knew to be the same age as the band.

For the Skool trilogy, the band focused on themes important to that age group – bullying, exams and studying, young love, parents. "We tried to relate with listeners who are of our age group and brought up topics that we could think about together," explained Suga. "The pain and uncertainty associated with being young, and the wrong ideas that can form during that age were issues we wanted to put in our songs." J-Hope agreed: "BTS makes music to speak to the feelings of teenagers. To stop against the prejudice and oppression of the world for teenagers."

NO MORE DREAMING

BTS's first single to set the scene of their huge ambitions was "No More Dream". The song was released in South Korea on 13 June 2013, the day after the album dropped. It has been described as "an ode to teen apathy, a rebellious rejection of Korean traditionalism". The track reached No.14 in the Billboard World Digital Charts – it would be one of the last times a song of theirs would place so low in the charts.

With Big Hit Entertainment, an independent record label,

distributing the song, and not a Korean major label such as SM, YG, or JYP, the track suffered from a critical failure to reach fans – an audience who Bang felt were in need of a band like BTS. "At that time BTS was coming out of my needs and the market's needs. Nowadays, people want more than just skills. They want their idols to have some sort of aura of an artist. Kids that you don't have to teach how to express themselves, they just need to take it out and show what's inside of them." He continued: "I recently came across a document from 2012, the year before BTS debuted, in which we were debating what kind of idol group to create. It said, 'What kind of hero is the youth of today looking for?' Not someone who dogmatically preaches from above. Rather, it seems like they need a hero who can lend them a shoulder to lean on, even without speaking a single word." The collective personalities of the seven members of BTS fit this description rather accurately, so Bang felt.

Following the release of 2 Cool 4 Skool in 2013, BTS began starring in their own SBS MTV variety show called Rookie King: Channel Bangtan as well as broadcasting their very own show, called American Hustle Life, in which the seven members begin to understand the ways of American hip-hop by speaking with US hip-hop stars such as Coolio. "The members like hip-hop music. We set out to protect the value of K-pop's distinctiveness that was made in the '90s. Visually beautiful, creating music as a package, and a group that is cool on stage. This surpasses language. Upon this we added BTS's unique value along with hip-hop music. These two things lowered the entry barrier to western markets. K-pop is unfamiliar to westerners but they are familiar with hip-hop music." The band's love of hip-hop would also broaden the band's individual tastes and would help push the band toward a more mature sound, as heard on their next Korean album, Dark & Wild. "'Dark & Wild'? That's what the group is!" RM would explain…

Showing off their choreography skills at MBC Music's 'Show Champion', Ilsan, September 10, 2014.

MIN YOON-GI

Min Yoon-gi, or Suga, to his fans, raps as sweet as his name suggests. His first love is hip-hop, followed by his habit of wearing Jungkook's underwear and doing absolutely nothing on his days off, hence the nickname Motionless Min. Suga is a free-flowing rhyme kingpin and rap master, a skill he has perfected since a very young age. "I have been writing rhymes and lyrics since I was a kid," Suga has explained. "They are all the little minor feelings and thoughts that go through my mind. I shuffle them a year or so later, and they become great lyrics for songs."

ABOVE Suga at the American Music Awards, Los Angeles, November 19, 2017.

OPPOSITE Suga made a great first impression at BTS's debut showcase in 2013.

"I was born in Daegu in the South, the fourth biggest city of Korea, and grew up there until I came up to Seoul," Suga revealed in an interview. "When I was young, I was pretty much an ordinary kid... until I started to be interested in music in the fifth year of elementary school."

It was at this time that hip-hop began to fill Suga's ears, influencing the young musician's mind with ideas of becoming a hip-hop star in his own right. He invented his first alter-ego, going by the name of Gloss, composing beats in his hometown of Deagu, and giving them away to local artists. His skills became noticed following the track of Reflow's that he produced, entitled "Who Am I".

"Along with listening to music, I also started writing music at the same time," he explained. "It wasn't like someone told me to do it, I just did it. I started writing rap lyrics in elementary school and started composing after I went to middle school. Back then, no one around me liked hip-hop. It is extremely popular in Korea now, but when I first started listening to it, no one else was. I thought that there probably wasn't anyone else on the streets who rapped, except for me." With his love of hip-hop fuelling Suga's ambitions, the young rapper began seeking out a crew who could help him focus his talents. "In my first year of high school, I joined a hip-hop crew called 'D-town' and began rapping properly. I have been rapping since elementary school, but since there wasn't anyone who raps around me, I thought I was the best." It was only when Suga (as Gloss) discovered the local Daegu underground hip-hop scene in his early teens that he met like-minded souls who got high on hip-hop. It was also where Suga's life changed forever.

"I knew Big Hit was holding an audition in Daegu," Suga said of the Big Hit competition called "Hit it", which he had seen promoted on a flyer. He decided to go for it. "I went there knowing nothing except that it was a company formed by composer Bang Si-hyuk. I auditioned and I was told that I was accepted the next day. I wanted to debut and become a singer doing my music as a trainee. There was never a moment when I didn't have a dream to do that."

Born on 9 March 1993, Suga is one of the fiercely independent and talented creative assets in BTS, alongside RM, as well as an advocate of raising serious questions about society and justice in his lyrics. In short, Suga is a true artist. "I have no greed of being recognized," he stated. "I just want to make music. I don't have an interest towards the entertainment world too – everyone says they want to act, or to go on variety shows, but I don't want to do those. I want to be the best rapper, the best producer. I have to try."

"IN ADDITION TO BEING WHAT WE ARE AS BTS, WE WANTED TO BRING SOME CHANGES AND WE ACTUALLY WANTED TO EVOLVE AS A GROUP. WE WANTED TO SHOW OUR MANY COLOURS, BUT WE STILL WANT TO CONSOLE OTHERS AND GIVE HOPE TO OTHERS." SUGA

DARK & WILD

With BTS's first *Skool* trilogy out in the wild, it was time for the group to commence with the next chapter of their career – their *Youth* trilogy, a period of music that evolved into more experimental, more high-energy dance-music territory. The band were growing up alongside their fans and their music had to represent that. Between 2015 and 2016, the boys defined their Youth trilogy with their first full-length album *Dark & Wild* and their first mega-hit single 'I NEED U' from their EP *The Most Beautiful Moment in Life, Part 1*. The adventure was only just beginning...

TRACKLISTING:
Intro: What Am I To You
Danger (Lead single)
War of Hormone
Hip-hop Lover
Let Me Know
Rain
BTS Cypher Pt.3: Killer (ft. Supreme Boi)
Interlude: What Are You Doing
Can You Turn Off Your Phone?
Blanket Kick
24/7 = Heaven
Look Here
Second Grade
Outro: Does That Make Sense?

DARK&WILD

ABOVE Suga, Jin, Jungkook and RM sit down for once, and discuss their debut album Dark & Wild at the Samsung Card Hall, Seoul, August 19, 2014.

OPPOSITE The group wow the audience on MTV's *The Show* at SBS Prism Tower, Seoul, June 30, 2015.

SKOOL'S OUT

With their *Skool* years behind them, BTS decided to walk a new path musically. While *2 Cool 4 Skool* had introduced the hip-hop and rap elements, and the individual personalities of the band, the group's sound was proving too niche to generate a crossover hit. And the boys wanted a hit!

So, in 2015, BTS – together with Bang, and producer P-Dogg – began writing and recording more upbeat dance tracks with lyrics that would resonate with the transforming age group of their fans. Puberty was long gone. It was time to dance! These would be the songs that would define their *Youth* trilogy.

"BTS music is based on hip-hop and pop music in general, because all the members grew up listening to famous hip-hop artists as well as pop vocalists, even before the debut. It was definitely very hip-hop back in 2013, and the style kind of evolved as we grew up listening to and experiencing many different genres of music the last couple of years," explained RM of their musical shift. "We constantly look for new beats and read books just to intrigue ourselves to renovate as artists, even if it means failure to some of us. It is part of the band's experiment to evolve together as an entity to make the better, newer music. Thus we don't want to label our music as a certain genre or limit it to K-pop."

With *Dark & Wild* established as the theme for their first full-length record, BTS collectively began to be inspired by Bang's freedom of allowing them to write "the music you want to create."

As leader, RM sought to express a lot of thoughts through his perspective as a singer and man, no longer a teenager. "I wanted to express the thoughts of men in their early twenties."

The album was titled *Dark & Wild* as a foundation from which to explore two themes often considered by young men emerging into adulthood – darkness and wildness, the idea of a reckless and carefree youth that leads to growing up and falling into temptation. "'*Dark & Wild*' came out as we talked with Bang," revealed RM. "At first, it was kind of hard to place the words of '*Dark & Wild*' to BTS. However, I thought a lot about it, and our music criticizes the bad points of society and pokes fun at it a lot. I thought that that side of us was dark. And we also always wore dark clothes."

Dark & Wild was visualized, conceptually, as a record of two halves, listened to all at once, as opposed to individual songs listened to out of order. By doing this, the band were free to explore lyrical themes that would complement one another and fill one like a cohesive story. "We created the tracklist from the start to the end with the thought that fans would listen to it from start to finish. There's an interlude in the middle, so you can see that interlude as a midpoint where the 'dark' would be the songs in the middle and afterwards it would be 'wild'."

The album's lead single, "Danger", promoted the album's two themes perfectly, especially alongside the accompanying music video that sees the band dressed in black performing with tight

BTS encourage their audience to fly away with them at a *Wings* promotion, November 27, 2015.

choreography in a subway tunnel and a warehouse with burning shopping carts! Very dark and wild!

The album's dual themes also allowed the band the scope to express themselves across a wide platform of subjects, lyrically. "Compared to other groups, our group is quite heavy on the lyrics," said RM of the album's release. "Since there are a lot of things we want to say."

Dark & Wild debuted at the No. 2 spot on the Gaon charts in South Korea, the band's highest chart placement at the time. Triumphant, BTS knew that their gamble of a new musical direction had worked. However, it wasn't until the release of "I NEED U", from *The Most Beautiful Moment in Life, Part 1* EP, six months later, in April 2015, that the lives of BTS truly changed forever.

"BTS as a group took off with the success of our hit single 'I NEED U,'" RM told *Time* magazine. The video garnered more than a million views in 24 hours and gave BTS the jolt of confidence they needed. As a result of the song's success, the band went to KCON, a K-pop music festival, in America and Europe in 2015, completely buoyed by their sonic reinvention. "We didn't realize we were becoming famous until the KCON festival," said RM.

"Thousands of fans were calling our name at the venue, and almost everyone memorized the Korean lyrics of our songs, which was amazing and overwhelming. Who would have thought that people from across the ocean, Europe, the US, South America – even Tahiti – would love our songs and performances, just by watching them on YouTube? We were just grateful... and we still are."

From this moment on, the band's fan base grew exponentially and they embarked on a massive world tour as *The Most Beautiful Moment in Life, Pt. 2* hit the Top Ten in international music charts, including Billboard's World Albums chart, becoming the first K-pop band ever to achieve such an accomplishment. As ever, RM understood why BTS were making waves where other K-pop bands failed. It was all about the brotherly bond between the band. "Our chemistry that fans can feel from performance and behind the scene videos, and sincerity, music, and high-quality performance are all mixed into a powerful weapon," he explained. "It destroys the language barrier and makes fans request our songs to radio stations."

Fame and stardom had arrived... but no-one, not even Bang or RM, could have predicted the level of success that came next...

ABOVE BTS dominate the 2015 Melon Music Awards in Seoul, November 7, 2015.

BELOW The group fly through their moves at the Melon Music Awards. Can anyone guess the song?

JUNG HO-SEOK

Jung Ho-seok, or J-Hope, is BTS's ray of sunshine, the group's best dancer (maybe!) who adopted his stage name simply because he wanted to be a source of light and hope to his fans. Jin, his closest band mate, says of him: "He's a kid who's just all hope. He makes anyone bright when he's with them – he laughs even when there's no reason."

Before joining BTS in 2012, J-Hope, the "mother of BTS" according to other band members, was part of an underground street dance team called Neuron. It was while with this dance troupe that J-Hope developed his love of body-popping, a dance move which not only showcases J-Hope's mastery of dancing but also his versatility and energy. "While promoting underground with my street dance team, I did a lot of popping," revealed J-Hope in 2013. "In popping, there's another sub-genre called Boogaloos and that was the one I did the most. I got a lot of prizes and performed a lot. Rap Monster rapped underground; I danced."

Born in Gwangju on 18 February 1994, J-Hope was inspired to a live a life full of dancing during middle school when he watched western music videos on the fledgling YouTube. "When I was a little

"THE MUSIC HELPED ME SYMPATHIZE WITH OUR YOUNG GENERATION AND ALSO EMPATHIZE WITH THEM. I'D LIKE TO CREATE AND WRITE MORE MUSIC THAT REPRESENTS THEM." J-HOPE

kid, I simply loved music and enjoyed expressing myself with my body. Everyone liked me when I went up on the stage at a talent search in elementary school, and that's when I decided to become a music artist."

Following his time in Neuron, J-Hope built up a reputation as a dancer with a bright future, winning a national dance competition in South Korea in 2008. "While enrolling at Korea Arts School, there were lots of trainees coming from different districts," J-Hope revealed. "When I debuted with Bangtan, my friends said, 'J-Hope, is he the one from that dance academy in Gwangju?' That's how famous I was!"

Dancing was J-Hope's dream, and in order to live the dream he had to struggle, just like the other members of the band, during the trainee stages of pledging themselves to Big Hit Entertainment. "My goal was always clear. To stand on stage, to become the best," revealed J-Hope. "But first, I needed to survive. The trainee period was a constant cycle of having to survive. When one person entered, one person would have to leave. I had to withstand that."

Legends tell that J-Hope nearly got left out of BTS, for not being quite the right fit, but RM persuaded the people in charge at Big Hit that BTS needed J-Hope. They listened; and the rest is history. J-Hope thanked his band mate. "RM's the type of person who'd take care of you at the right moment."

TOP J-Hope before the stardom at the group's debut showcase, 2013.

ABOVE Giving hope to all his fans with his sweet dancing J-Hope!

WINGS

Today, thanks to the worldwide success of *Wings*, BTS have begun to mean more to their growing ARMY than ever before. And like Beatlemania that dominated the globe in the previous century, BTS-mania has its eyes set on world domination. Despite a language barrier, BTS made it happen. It all began right here, and right now, with *Wings*.

In 2016, *Wings* became the first K-pop album to crack the Top 30 of the American Billboard charts. It was the seismic event that BTS and Big Hit had been waiting for. It was the moment where everybody's hard work, punishing schedules and sacrifice came together. "I don't think the successful result of *Wings* was expected," admitted Bang. "But I don't think the results were a matter of luck. The members have steadily taken steps and they are showing the results of their continuous growth to the public."

To the band, success outside of Korea was shocking. A complete "WTF!" moment. "I was shocked to see our team name in the Hot 100 chart," RM said. "In the United States, a song that breaks into the Top 40 is considered a nationwide hit, you know. The fact that we were in the Top 30 was just unbelievable."

With *Wings*, BTS had learnt to fly over oceans and into the homes of the historically difficult US record-buying public. Many bands over several decades have tried and failed, crashing and

TRACKLISTING:
Intro: Boy Meets Evil
Blood Sweat & Tears
Begin
Lie
Stigma
First Love
Reflection
MAMA
Awake
Lost
BTS Cypher 4
Am I Wrong
21st Century Girls
Two! Three! (Wishing for
    Better Days)
Interlude: Wings

"EACH SONG ON WINGS REFLECTS THE HARDSHIPS WE OVERCAME. IT REALLY REPRESENTS THE PERSONS WE ARE." RM

All in a row on the red carpet at the 25th Seoul Music Awards, Olympic Park, January 14, 2016

KCON 2016. Day 2. BTS perform one of their first, and historic, US shows. New Jersey, June 25, 2016

burning; the elusive US market was a beast and often proved too big and too fragmented to be beaten. But BTS had done it. The second continent had fallen.

The concept for the *Wings* album was vital to the record's success. It set the mood at the right time; it was not only a creative, artistic and sonic leap forward for the septet, it also did the unthinkable: it featured seven solo tracks that showcased the personality of each member. *Who else but BTS does that?*

The theme of the album is formed around the concept of young men, of a similar age to the band members, resisting/ accepting temptation and losing their innocence, a concept building chronologically onwards from BTS's previous *Youth* trilogy period, which culmimated in the *Dark & Wild* album. This concept allowed the band to have a freedom to explore more individual stories and allowed the personality of each member to shine through on those individual stories.

"For the *Wings* album, we are telling side stories from seven different perspectives," said RM. "We wanted to show different looks with sweet hair colour changes to look younger, brighter and warmer too."

The decision was made that each member would write and compose their own solo song, in which the member could reveal their own story scene and their own outlook on life based around the album's core theme.

"We try to tell our stories/thoughts in the songs," explained RM. "Fans empathize with our songs because they go through similar phases in life. Making the solo tracks on the album was quite a venture, but it's connected to the concept. Like, when you watch the 'I NEED U' video, everyone has their own crises and characters. It's connected to our real personalities and characters, but the solo songs have their own characters and personalities. It's all connected. It's a mixture and that's why fans get interested in the concepts."

Wings' lead single "Blood Sweat & Tears" defines the concept. "The song relays an optimistic determination to use our wings to go far, even if we are met with temptations in life," revealed Suga. "The harder a temptation is to resist, the more you think about it. That uncertainty is part of the process of growing. 'Blood Sweat & Tears' is a song that shows how one thinks, chooses, and grows," concluded RM.

KCON 2016 USA

Each of the band's solo songs come together under an umbrella of different musical styles to create a cohesive foundation, but they also showcase each member's evolving transformation from who they used to be and who they want to be.

RM's musing on his track "Reflection" displays a new side to the rapper, and a tightened style of lyrical delivery; Suga's "First Love" is almost a spoken-word track with the rapper tripping down memory lane about his first love at elementary school; J-Hope's spiky hip-hop infused track "MAMA" speaks of his mother's tenacity being like a "breaking ball" while the singalong chorus jumps and jumps to the refrain of "Hey Mama" – it's a live favourite to watch out for; Jin wakes up and belts out a ballad with his "Awake" tune; and Jimin sings his heart out on the booming pop hit "Lie", which raced ahead of the group's other solo efforts on the iTunes download charts when the album was released. As an album, *Wings* is defined by the sum of all its separate, but equal, parts. Whereas RM once took on the responsibility of leader, now each member has stepped up to the mic with something important and meaningful to say too. BTS will always sound like they are having fun, but with *Wings*, they began to sound vital. "The big thing about creating our universe is expandability," explains Suga of the band's constantly evolving sound, style and sonics. "Because our universe we create draws from our personal lives and interests. We can expand it as much as we want and it's not alien for us. Having that allows us more diversity in the stories we can tell and the music we can make."

ABOVE Suited and booted at New Jersey's KCON 2016. The band were dressed to impress their new US fans.

OPPOSITE Looking "hella lit" at Mnet's 'M Count Down', CJ E&M Center, Seoul, July 4, 2013.

"WHEN I GET QUESTIONS ABOUT WHY IS K-POP SO POPULAR, I ALWAYS TELL THEM K-POP IS LIKE A GREAT MIX OF MUSIC, VIDEOS, VISUALS, CHOREOGRAPHY, SOCIAL MEDIA AND REAL-LIFE."
RM

KIM NAM-JOON

Every boy band needs a captain, a member who leads the group to success. The Beatles had John, NSYNC had Justin, Take That have Gary. For BTS, it is, of course, RM, aka Kim Nam-joon. Formerly known as the underground rapper Runch Randa, RM is the group's principal songwriter, producer and rapper, responsible for their taut and glossy melodies and inspirational/ aspirational lyrics. In 2018, following the release of his solo mixtape, and a huge fanbase all to himself, RM is a multi-talented and respected composer with a fame beyond all the stars. But to the rest of the band, he is, of course, just one of the Bangtan boys.

"PEOPLE LOVE ME FOR WHAT I AM. THAT'S HOW I MANAGE TO BE ME AND BE HUMBLE AS A HUMAN BEING." RM

RM was the first member to be discovered by Big Hit Entertainment in 2010 and the first to be recruited for BTS following his audition with Bang Si-hyuk, the founder/CEO of Big Hit. "RM is extremely self-reflective, sophisticated and philosophical, considering his age," the mogul would say at the time.

It soon became clear that RM was not just your ordinary rapper-songwriter. The 1.8-m (6-ft) tall boy with "shiny hair" and an IQ of 148 – near genius level! – was a star waiting for his chance to shine. "Back in 2010, I was introduced to Bang. I was an underground rapper and only 16 years old, a freshman at high school. Bang thought I had potential as a rapper and lyricist."

In 2007, at the age of just 13, the rapper was beginning to explore his talent for expressing himself lyrically as part of the rap crew DaeNamHyup, a group that consisted of other high-profile underground rappers. RM wasn't alone on the underground scene. Suga and J-Hope were with him too, the three of them exploring Korea's underground music scene, and its potential to become globally recognized, together. They were the "first three" to join BTS. "We came together with a common dream to write, dance and produce music that reflects our musical backgrounds as well as our life values of acceptance, vulnerability and being successful," RM said. RM continued to write and perform his songs, building up a library of lyrics and melodies that, in a few years' time, would define BTS's energetic dance-pop hip-hop act.

The world had never seen such an act as BTS before. And at the centre of the band's success is RM. "I started this because I wanted to say something. There was a message inside me and I wanted to spread it as music," the rapper revealed. "But we're just a normal group of boys from humble backgrounds who have a lot of passion and a dream to be famous. The seven of us have pushed each other to be the best we can be for the last four years. It has made us as close as brothers."

RM is the figure at the heart of the world's love affair with K-pop, a talent who has proven that being the leader of a boy band doesn't mean he's just a celebrity; RM is an artist and role model who will ensure he and his band not only enjoy the ride they are on but are also taken seriously too. "Through the prism of my songs I constantly observe society and I want to be a person who can have a better, positive impact on other people. It will always be important to keep working hard, dancing better, writing better songs, touring and setting an example."

OPPOSITE RM also expresses himself through his range of unique fashion style and looks.

LEFT An inspirational figure to millions, RM speaks to fans at KCON 2016.

PARK JI-MIN

The final member to join BTS, Jimin is known as the cutest member of the band (but don't tell the others...!). As V once said of his beloved band mate: "Jimin is a real piece of cuteness, like the youngest in the family." Forever showing off his impeccable stomach muscles and even more perfect vocal pitch, Jimin is a perfectionist when it comes to his dance choreography and his singing.

Born in the city of Busan, on 13 October 1995, Park Ji-min – or Jimin, as the world now calls him – prior to joining BTS was enrolled at Busan High School of Arts studying theatre and film. He was regarded as one of the school's top modern dance students. Such was Jimin's natural talent as a dancer, his teachers at school urged him to audition for Big Hit Entertainment. At school, Jimin's "future dreams" of what career he wanted to follow would change every day. One day he wanted to be a chef, the next a pirate. As with the other members of BTS, Jimin discovered his love of dance and performance during his time at school. He would practise every day after his studies were finished, building up the confidence to attend the local dance academy in 2010. "Whenever I had time, I would practise dance. During high school, I spared no effort in dancing. At the time, my friends and I only knew dancing, we got together and practised, messed around and then continued to practise."

When his opportunity to join on the dotted line at Big Hit Entertainment came along, after passing his audition to become a trainee, Jimin moved from his hometown to live in Seoul. "The most difficult part of the trainee life was the uncertainty of my future," revealed Jimin. "I was the last to be added to the group, that's why I practise so hard. I got anxious when I hear "you might get eliminated this time", so I wanted to do my best with practising. If I practised until 4am, I would sleep a bit and go practise singing at 6am for an hour and then go to school. This routine continued for about a year. At the time, I've never thought I could become a member of BTS, but I was chosen, but only as a substitute member. The rest of the chosen members said, 'We want to debut with Jimin,' and that became my strength."

Due to his natural rhythm and perfectionist attitude, Jimin's time as a trainee was the shortest out of all the members (just under a year – Jungkook took three!) and once Jimin was in the band, the line-up was complete. Jimin was the final piece of the puzzle.

"I was so excited when we debuted," remembers Jimin. "After the showcase we all cried." With the group's first taste of worldwide success on the *Wings* album, it was Jimin's track "Lie" that was the standout solo track, a hot slice of majestic pop, that highlighted Jimin's singing ability more than fans had heard before.

LEFT Jimin isn't afraid to show his fashionable side!

OPPOSITE Jimin is thankful to the ARMY for attending the American Music Awards in Los Angeles, at the prestigious Microsoft Theater, November 19, 2017.

"I WOULD LOVE IT IF THEY REMEMBERED US AS BOYS WHO ALWAYS WANTED TO SHOW THEIR SINCERITY AND THEIR SINCEREST SIDE."
JIMIN

LOVE YOURSELF: TEAR

Regarded as the "turning point" and "second chapter" of the boys' rise to icon status, *Love Yourself: Tear*, released in May 2018 (the same month as their incredible win at the Billboard Music Awards) would see the band jump up to a whole new level of fame. Suddenly a boy band rapping in Korean was knocking American artists off the US Billboard charts. The world had turned upside down. The Bangtan Boys were back in town... and they had made it clear: they were here to stay...

BREAKING THE STATES

With *Wings*, BTS scored a record that landed not only on top of the Korean album charts but also within the Top 30 of the US Billboard charts, going on to receive two gold certifications for album sales. It also paved the way for *Love Yourself: Tear* to tear up all the previous records... and set new ones. The band were breaking records for their music, but they were also breaking language and stereotype boundaries too, proving that you can be a successful band without "embodying the Anglo-pop star ideal". In other words, BTS looked like no other band in the US or European charts... and, all of a sudden, the mainstream American record-buying public didn't mind. BTS had pushed the envelope. No other Korean act in history has ever managed that. And for BTS to be achieving all this success outside of the "big players" of the Korean music industry (such as YG and SM Entertainment) was even more unbelievable. BTS had become the golden boys of the worldwide charts all from the small independent offices of Big Hit Entertainment. Only today, they're not so small!

In order to help them make a bigger impact in the US, the boys decided to work with Steve Aoki, the most *en vogue* DJ of the day. If anything and anyone could help BTS break the States true and proper, it was a remix from Aoki.

In November 2017, the DJ worked his trap-beat magic on the group's "Mic Drop" from the *Love Yourself: Her* sessions. In doing so, Aoki gave BTS their first Top 40 hit single in the US and the perfect visibility boost ahead of the band's Billboard Music Awards and

RIGHT The band strike a perfect pose in the press room at the American Music Awards in Los Angeles, November 19, 2017.

"EVERYTHING AROUND BTS MOVES SO FAST, LIKE MAKING TEN SONGS IN HALF A YEAR. SOMETIMES IT'S TOO MUCH, BUT I ALWAYS REMIND MYSELF OF THINGS BACK IN 2007, I STARTED THIS BECAUSE I WANTED TO SAY SOMETHING. THERE WAS A MESSAGE INSIDE ME AND I WANTED TO SPREAD IT AS MUSIC." RM

American Music Awards performance of "DNA" that same month. All of a sudden, US pop ears were tuned to BTS, and their prolific back catalogue started seeing movement up the worldwide charts. "With 'Mic Drop' we dropped the mic and chapter one is over," exclaimed RM. What on earth could come next?

TAKING HOME TROPHIES

2017 saw the band reach the zenith of US success... so far. First up, in May 2017, the band collected the award for Top Social Artist at the prestigious Billboard Awards. "Everyone in the group was very nervous," the band reported on the night. "Some of us had to go to the men's room several times during the show. It was probably the most intense moment of our professional lives since our debut in 2013."

To celebrate the night and mark the occasion, Big Hit Entertainment released a statement that read: "It is such an honour for BTS and Big Hit Entertainment to be invited to the American Music Awards as one of the performers. Our partners in the US have helped us pave the way in every way possible, and together we are making history."

Indeed, history was made. Though when BTS's name was read aloud, no-one could quite believe it! "Once I heard 'BTS!' I honestly blacked out for a second and came back to myself," remembers RM. "I had prepared a little speech on my own because I thought we had a 20 per cent chance of winning out of five nominees. I really cannot remember what happened after that short acceptance speech on stage because everything felt like a dream from then on. On stage, the rapper announced proudly: "We won the Top Social Artist Award thanks to the dedication from our ARMY around the world. Our honour and gratitude must go directly to them."

By winning the Top Social Artist award, BTS broke Justin Bieber's six-year streak of collecting it. The win may have come as a shock to the band, but the ARMY knew their favourite band would win. In

order to do so, the ARMY voted for the #BTSBBMAs hashtag more than 320 million times!

"The official stats are in," tweeted RM, "and it's 320 million votes, which is amazing. We're so grateful for all the attention we're getting since the BBMAs and trying to realize it is actually real! It's good to be noticed worldwide, and we feel honoured to be nominated and win the award."

Since their Billboard Music Awards appearance, the name BTS was seen everywhere, from radio reports to newspaper articles to blogs discussing the arrival of "that boy band from South Korea" – an entirely new phenomenon that no pundit or popular culture vulture in the west had spoken of before. BTS were proof, if it were needed, that the internet was now the principal domain where music was discovered and made large.

But, of course, the triumphs didn't end there. Six months later, in November 2017, BTS were back on US soil to perform at the American Music Awards – the first Korean boy band ever to do so. Of course, they performed "DNA" – its lyric of "We've found our destiny" ringing out loud and proud.

ABOVE The winners of Top Social Artist at the 2018 Billboard Music Awards: BTS.

BELOW The band reveal *Love Yourself: Tear* to the world

LOVE YOURSELF 轉 Tear

ABOVE The world listens! BTS proudly accept the Top Social Artist award at the 2018 Billboard Music Awards, Las Vegas, May 20, 2018.

BELOW The 5th Gaon Chart K-Pop Awards saw the band in a playful mood – business as usual! February 17, 2016.

Millions of fans around the world watched BTS perform on *Jimmel Kimmel Live*, November 15, 2017.

ABOVE On the edge of their seats at the 2017 American Music Awards, November 19, 2017.

OPPOSITE The band return from their world tour to attend the 2017 Melon Music Awards in Seoul, December 2, 2017.

"The AMAs were the biggest gift we could have gotten from our fans," said Suga. "I grew up watching the awards show on the internet, since it was not available on TV. I felt so proud to be on the show and couldn't believe we performed on stage just prior to Diana Ross, who received the lifetime achievement award."

AND THEN THERE WAS HER

Released after the EP *Love Yourself: Her* and the Japanese album *Face Yourself*, *Love Yourself: Tear* was the full-length album of this period and the gift the ARMY had been waiting for expectantly. Naturally, it was to become the biggest-selling album in pre-orders ever, with over a million sales at home alone.

With the single "DNA" from the *Love Yourself: Her* sessions, BTS became the first K-pop group to attain more than 10, 20 and 100 million YouTube views. "DNA" is taking BTS to new ground, said RM in the moment. "We tried to apply new grammar and perspectives. If you listen to the song, you'll understand what I'm trying to say, it's very different from our previous music, technically and musically. I believe it's going to be the starting point of a second chapter of our career; the beginning of our Chapter Two."

The mini-album reached No. 14 on the UK album chart, went Top 10 on the US Billboard album chart and shot "DNA" to No. 67 on the Billboard Hot 100 – an accomplishment no other Korean pop group had ever achieved. And may never achieve... "This EP will mark the turning point of BTS," said RM at the time. It was also a watershed moment for the group in terms of wish fulfillment. The band's ARMY of fans suddenly multiplied, and the group pay close attention – really listen – to their fans. So, the more the ARMY grows, the louder BTS's voice gets. "Our fans, the 'ARMY', tell us about their feelings, failures, passions and

struggles all the time," explained RM. "We are inspired by them, because we try to write about how real young people – like the seven of us – face real-life issues. Most of our music is about how we perceive the world and how we try to persist as normal, average human beings. So, our fans inspire us and give us a direction to go as musicians. And of course, their love and support keeps us going."

This support allowed the group to pivot slightly and begin introducing more adult elements to their raps, giving their glossy tunes a hidden depth, as reflected on *Love Yourself: Her*. "The concept of The Most Beautiful Moment in Life [the band's previous mini-album] – that was chapter one for us," said RM following the release of *Love Yourself: Her*. "It feels like that because we were starting from the bottom, but on this concept, *Love Yourself*, we started to talk about some brighter things, like the real things in life. Professionally, we got on the Billboard and UK charts, and our stadiums are getting bigger... so both inside and outside, it's a turning point for BTS. I'd like to say we're just in a different universe now, I think, like a crab, we got a new shell."

THE TEAR DROP EXPLODES

With *Love Yourself: Tear*, there was a sense of just how important this phase in their career is now that the band are no longer searching for stardom. It found them. The next step is, obviously, to think about what kind of icons BTS want to be, and not let fame distract them from their true focus – entertaining and encouraging their fans to "love themselves". And this is why the *Love Yourself* concept is so important to the band – it's a stepping-stone for the band to discuss a wider range of important emotions. "Basically, love is complex," stated RM. "There's sort of some sides that make us really feel bad or depressed. There could be tears, there could be sadness. So, this time we wanted to focus on some of the parts of love that we want to run away from. So, the name is "Tear". The concept this time around, it's about honesty and love," RM divulged. "Sometimes we just turn away from some sort of situations, because in love and life, it's not like a fairytale. We always have a dark side, so we want to talk about like, the dark sides of love." "It's kind of deep," he concluded. "This album, [the storyline shows] if you're not too sure of yourself, your love won't last. You will see it in the choreography and the lyrics," RM shared, before revealing the theme's personal significance.

Love Yourself: Tear debuted at No. 1 on the US billboard charts upon its release in May 2018. Even Bang was surprised! "I thought of how great it would be if they could enter the top 100 of the Billboard 200 album chart, since their previous album *The Most Beautiful Moment in Life, Pt. 2* made it up to 171," said Bang. "We were shocked when the first week results came in. We recognized the explosive response from western fans and realized that there is still further room for growth for the boy band."

THE ANSWER

"I FEEL LIKE WE'RE A BALLOON. WE DON'T KNOW WHERE THAT BALLOON IS GOING, BUT I'M JUST TRYING TO ENJOY IT BECAUSE THERE WAS SO MUCH SUFFERING BEFORE. I'M TRYING NOT TO LOSE SIGHT OF WHAT WE'RE DOING." RM

The fourth and final release in the *Love Yourself* anthology, following 2017's *Love Yourself: Her* EP, April's *Love Yourself: Wonder* video and May 2018's *Tear*, *Love Yourself: Answer* is the springboard release before the band go out on the *Love Yourself* tour, their largest worldwide adventure on the road to date. Released in August 2018, the album, naturally, smashed as many records as its predecessors...

Released in four different versions, titled *S, E, L,* and *F. Love Yourself: Answer* contains seven new songs. The killer lead single "Idol" is the perfect representation of the album's ambitions – mixing traditional Korean culture and music mixed with trap beats and electronic dance music. The song, naturally, broke the internet within hours of its release. "The song has the message of loving one's true self no matter what others say," said J-Hope. Not content with releasing just one version of the song, BTS dropped a remix version of "Idol" with one of their own idols – US rap superstar Nicki Minaj. "We thought the song would come alive with Nicki Minaj's rapping, so we sent a request," said RM. "Nicki Minaj's side accepted, so it came to be!"

The music video accompanying the song set the YouTube record for most views in 24 hours, beating Taylor Swift's "Look What You Made Me Do", with more than 45 million views! The cheeky and energetic video, which sees the band bring together Korean traditions with the modern day, deserves every single view. "With our *Love Yourself* series we wanted to show the emotional development of a young man through love" explained RM. "We tried to send the message that loving yourself is where true love begins. For *Love Yourself: Answer* we have seven brand-new tracks. We've put our Korean traditional sound, performance and traditional Korean choreography into the videos too. This album is a celebration of our culture."

KIM TAE-HYUNG

Kim Tae-hyung is known to his beloved Bangtan Boys as, simply, V. While the rest of the band were either established rappers or up-and-coming dancers, known on the South Korean underground scene, V was an unknown at the time of becoming a trainee at Big Hit Entertainment. Nothing could be further from the truth now...

"I was born in Daegu, the same place as Suga," V recalled in an interview. "At elementary school, I was a curious kid who wanted to do everything. I lived in the countryside so I didn't imagine doing anything except for farming in the future, but I still thought I had to study hard. That changed after I fell in love with music. By the end of my sixth year at school, I had the dream of becoming a singer. It was my first time having a certain dream."

Unlike his six brothers in BTS, it is V who emerged from an upbringing where money was hard to come by, raised by his grandmother among a family of farmers. His dream was to pursue his love of music. It started with learning the saxophone at school, a skill he was encouraged to continue thanks to his father, who supported V's love of music and performing. "I started preparing for my dream from my first year of middle school. My father asked 'What do you want to do later?' and I answered 'I want to become a singer.' My father used to dream of becoming an actor, so after hearing my answer he told me very seriously 'If you want to become a singer, you have to learn at least one instrument.' So I learned saxophone for three years. It looks cool, but my lips hurt a lot and it was heavy too, it was quite hard."

One day after high school, V went to support a friend who was auditioning for Big Hit Entertainment to become a trainee. A member of the Big Hit rookie squad saw V in the waiting room and urged him to audition! V called his dad and asked for his permission to audition, and then walked into the room where all the Big Hit bigwigs were waiting. "I danced, rapped and showed my voice imitations and gags at the audition. I thought I would fail for sure but then they contacted me saying I passed. I thought it was a lie. I was the only one to pass that day in Daegu." The rest, well, is history!

Due to not being as well known on the underground music scene, V was kept hidden by Big Hit until the band's debut showcase. "After getting to debut, my existence was hidden until the end. I was the secret weapon! Because of that, there were times I couldn't say I was going to debut and was upset," revealed V. "The other members all had schedules, only I stayed behind at the dorm and rested... So when I was revealed, I was extremely happy. I was so happy thinking 'My dream since the sixth year of elementary school finally came true!'"

As a trainee, V met his future band mates, becoming firm friends with them fast. "I came up to Seoul in August, during my first year of high school, and went to the arts high school there, starting my trainee life. I was happy to even just become a trainee. I was able to dance every day, and I worked hard each and every day. At the time, the present was more important than a future that I couldn't see." Now that V is an invaluable member of the BTS squad, the singer, dancer and lover of art and photography counts his lucky stars that he had the confidence to wow the crowd at Big Hit on that fateful day of his friend's audition. "BTS is the first and the last team of my life. I want to keep going up together with the members to a high place until the end." V

"I'M JUST AN ORDINARY PERSON NEXT DOOR. I NEVER PRETEND TO BE SOMEONE I'M NOT." V

OPPOSITE V flicks his signature V!

RIGHT V and singer Bebe Rexha share the love at the 2018 Billboard Music Awards in Las Vegas May 20, 2018.

STYLE AND SUBSTANCE: THE EVOLUTION OF BTS

BTS love fashion (in particular, Gucci), clothes and colour. Throughout their tenure on top of the global charts, the band have presented many various styles, uniforms, outfits and disguises, as well as more hair colour changes than you can count on one hand. They are perfectionists when it comes to their clothes, so for your viewing pleasure, here are seven standout moments showcasing BTS's brilliant, if sometimes bizarre, fashion sense!

ABOVE Showcasing the first album *DARK & WILD* at Blue Square, Seoul, South Korea on August 19, 2014. The members of BTS showed off a stylish but rebellious denim and leather look, with chains and hair to match.

"IT'S SOMETIMES JUST UNBELIEVABLE; PARTIALLY MAYBE IT WAS A BIT OF LUCK. BUT WE DO OUR BEST AND KEEP WORKING NO MATTER WHAT. THE FANS SUPPORTED US SO MUCH, THEY LOVE US. WE'D LIKE TO GO HIGHER FROM HERE." JUNGKOOK

2013 INCHEON KOREAN MUSIC WAVE
인천한류관광콘서트 2014인천아시아경기대회 D-1년 기념 한류콘서트

RIGHT Black and gold bling, and muted hair colours showed BTS' were all about business at their very first 'Incheon Korean Music Wave' photo call in 2013. This would be the start of BTS-mania!

BELOW The magnificent seven look, well, magnificent at the 3rd Gaon Chart K-Pop Awards, Olympic Gym, Seoul, February 12, 2014.

gaon 가온 스타뉴스☆ *3rd* GAONCHART

ABOVE The septet went to work onstage in office attire for their performance at SBS MTV' *The Show*, June 30, 2015. One of their less extravagant fashion costumes – rarely to be seen again!

BELOW The group go back to their hip-hop roots with an urban-inspired look, while visiting their US fans in the home of their beloved hip-hop – New York City! March 22, 2017.

LEFT From hip-hop hipsters to proper-looking pop stars, BTS once again show a new thread to the fashion sense at the *Love Yourself: Her* press conference, September 17, 2018.

BELOW Dressed to kill in their suits – very suave and sophisticated! It can only mean one thing: they've gone to the Golden Disk Awards! January 10, 2018.

JEON JUNG-KOOK

▼
▼
▼

Jeon Jung-kook, or Jungkook, is BTS's maknae – the youngest member. One of the traditions of K-pop is that special attention is made toward the youngest in the group, showering them with praise, protection and affection. But, when you're as talented, funny and handsome as Jungkook, that adoration comes naturally anyway...

Before stardom and success came searching for this talented singer and dancer, Jungkook could be found studying at Baek Yang Middle School and, later, Seoul School of Performing Arts High School. It was while at school that Jungkook's star begin to shine. "In seventh grade, I dreamt of becoming a singer after listening to G-Dragon's songs. Then in eighth grade, after leaving the *Superstar K3* auditions, I got cast by Big Hit and became a part of Bangtan."

Jungkook may have been just 15 years old when he appeared at a BTS debut showcase in Seoul in 2013, but he was already one of the most in-demand singers in the country after auditioning for South Korean talent show, *Superstar K*. While he progressed no further in the show than the final elimination round ("I got eliminated anyway. Even if I had passed, I think I would have chosen Big Hit," Jungkook said, such was his desire to join BTS), Jungkook came to the attention of Bang Si-hyuk's Big Hit Entertainment and signed up with the agency as soon as he was offered that most prestigious of positions – trainee. He was aged just 12! Jungkook would be with the band as trainee for three years before making his debut alongside his BTS brothers.

However, according to Bang Si-hyuk, BTS's producer and CEO, Jungkook almost didn't debut with the band because of how shy he was when it came to singing. Apparently, every time he would sing, he would start to cry! A few years later, in 2018, when Jungkook took to the stage on *The Ellen DeGeneres Show*, or any one of the numerous awards shows the group were invited to, Jungkook's fears never returned. "I was never nervous," Jungkook exclaimed. "That's because I believe in our fans. In those moments, I felt I made the right choice to pursue a singing career, so why be scared?"

As was the case with many of the other members of BTS, it was RM's mad skills as a rapper and producer that most inspired Jungkook to join. Of course, RM was keen to pay back the praise. "It's Jungkook for me," said RM of his band mate's ability to become an icon. He's good at various things and doesn't lack in anything. He's good-looking, and he has a lot of ambition, so he's proficient in instruments and sports. He's good at everything."

"BREAKING NEW RECORDS IS IMPORTANT, BUT WHAT I WANT MOST IS TO CREATE PERFORMANCES AND MUSIC THAT WILL SATISFY OUR FANS."
JUNGKOOK

OPPOSITE Last, but not least, the baby of the band: Jungkook!

BELOW Jungkook's out in front as the boys perform at their 'Skool Luv Affair' showcase, Lotte Card Art Center, Seoul, February 11, 2014.

BEYOND THE STARS

Ever since the group made their first live appearance at the debut showcase in Seoul in 2013, BTS have been on the move. Every move has been followed and adored by BTS's loyal and loving ARMY of fans, supporting their favourite band with every release, every show, every tweet and every award. Without the ARMY, BTS would simply not exist. And it is with the band's extended touring around the world, that BTS get to reach out and speak to and meet their fans every night.

THE ARMY

Today, BTS are more than just a K-pop phenomenon – they are global icons, acclaimed for their record-smashing, barrier-breaking, trend-setting, dance-pop and hip-hop tunes. BTS's accessibility as a group has helped them connect with fans from all over the world through their distinct but seperate personalities. Today, the ARMY is K-pop's biggest fandom – EVER... Like Beatlemania that dominated the world in the previous century, BTS-mania is set to grow even bigger as the band conquers new territories around the world. ARMY, or "Adorable Representatives of M.C for Youth", power the band's energy, or, as RM puts it: "We are wings for one another. Let's fly together high up."

"It's very much an honour that we get power and attention from our fans when we use our voices more", continued RM. "It's important to us and the bigger the voice that we get, the more powerful that our words become." Well said, RM!

BEHIND THE SOCIAL

BTS's commitment to social media not only earned them Top Social Artist at the Billboard Music Awards in 2017 – thanks to more than 300 million tweets about the band – the band also use social media to connect and engage with their millions of fans every day. It was, after all, on YouTube where the band's career took off, following their prolific uploads to their channel. "We are a group that has benefited the most from social media," said RM. "It's an environment that doesn't limit us to Korea."

But BTS's social-media prowess does not just stem from the band's desire to grow their 16-million+ ARMY fanbase, or just talk about the music. The group's shared Twitter account –@bts_twt – is there to truly connect with their fans; it's a place for sharing. "We mostly interact with our Twitter messages by uploading selfies, [sharing] music recommendations and street-fashion photos, etc. It's about our daily life as a band on tour – and also as a group of

RIGHT RM takes a group selfie with the boys that will be shared millions of times on social media.

ABOVE BTS look ready to party at the 2018 Billboard Music Awards, Las Vegas, May 20, 2018. Big night!

BELOW Winners of the Top Social Artist award at the 2018 Billboard Music Awards!

silly friends who make fun of one another backstage. We don't really get to reply to fans on a regular basis, because there are just so many of them. But we do try to read all the reactions and replies. It's also always interesting and inspiring for us to see what they create for us," said RM. "It's not easy to run a social-media account over a long period of time, but we love communicating with our fans every day and night."

For their fans, the answer of why BTS have achieved worldwide success is simple. BTS are more than just a band – they are the symbol of freedom, the agents of change, the burst of kaleidoscopic colour in a musical landscape yearning for change. And the band aren't shy to express themselves... and give others hope. "Adults need to create policies that can facilitate that overall social change. Right now, the privileged class, the upper class, needs to change the way they think," said Suga. "And this isn't just Korea, but the rest of the world. The reason why our music resonates with people around the world who are in their teens, 20s and 30s is because of these issues. Moving past right and wrong, truth and falsehood, citizens coming together and raising their voices is something that we all actively support. If we don't talk about these issues, who will?"

Of course, as the band are acutely aware, with more fans, comes great responsibility. BTS are more than just singers, dancers, performers, entertainers – they are role models. "We would be lying if we said there wasn't any pressure in front of us. But we manage to get over it by openly talking about it with one another all the time. As you might know, we've been living together in the same house for the last five years, and we share literally everything even if it is stress and burden. BTS teamwork helps us get through the pressure and expectation in everyday life, and it also lets us stay humble as ordinary people – like guys next door. We make casual jokes and give pieces of advice to other members so that we can still be down-to-earth, as we were before 'BTS'." And that, in a nutshell, is why BTS are the best.

> **"MUSIC TRANSCENDS LANGUAGE. BTS COMMUNICATES WITH OUR FANS BY STAYING TRUE TO OURSELVES AND BELIEVING IN MUSIC EVERY DAY."**
> RM

BELOW BTS perform 'DNA' at the 2017 American Music Awards, November 19, 2017.

BURN THE STAGE: THE MOVIE!

Released on 15 November 2018, BTS's first feature-length film, *Burn the Stage*, gave the BTS ARMY an even more intimate and personal insight into their favourite Korean boy band. After five years of living in technicolour on small screens, or lit up by the ARMY's custom-made light sticks on stages all around the world, finally the band were given the chance to shine in 4K surround-sound on the big screen. The film would become 2018's greatest "global movie event".

Concluding a year that had rocketed the band higher than it ever thought possible – and from being a serious contender to a genuine global music superpower – 2018 had it all for BTS. Except sleep...!

October was the busiest month by far: RM released his second mixtape, *Mono*, to much fan praise; the group performed two songs ("I'm Fine" and "Idol") on the US most-watched talk-show, *The Tonight Show with Jimmy Fallon*; they announced news of a new English track "Waste It on Me" (with Steve Aoki); played massive shows at London's 02 Arena; and went viral with their appearance on *The Graham Norton Show* (a must watch on YouTube!) But it was the release of their first trailer of *Burn the Stage* on 23 October that truly sent the ARMY into mega-meltdown. This was the moment everyone was waiting for – a movie!

"A journey of 40 concerts across 19 countries with more than 550,000 roaring audience members, making history that gave wings to seven boys" – so read the accompanying press release to news of the movie. The two-minute trailer clocked up more than one million views on YouTube in one day. "We're proud that everything we do is giving off light." J-Hope said of the moment, humbly.

The ARMY, of course, knew that a feature-length film was inevitable: it was just a question of when. With their cinematic approach to their music videos, and love of acting, film flows through BTS's DNA. Indeed, the group's debut movie is not entirely new – rather, it is the condensing of their YouTube Red series of the same name, which began in March 2017. The series showed the band as no one concert could, offering access all areas, showcasing the group's dedication to one another, their music, and their global fan base, as they went around the world on their critically and commercially successful *Wings* tour. The docu-series shared a spotlight on a band of seven brothers as they became pop stars all over the world, and how they managed to keep it all together, together. After all, BTS have become the most-watched group on YouTube, amassing more than 10 billion views across 800 videos on their Bangtan TV channel.

Burn the Stage, the eight-part YouTube series, has been condensed and subtitled into an 85-minute movie for fans to understand no matter where they live, with added performances, extra behind-the-scenes footage and new "from the heart" interviews with all seven members. But, of course, this is just the first BTS film of many to come. The question is what will they show us next? What other ambitions do the band have set in their sights?

"I'm just throwing it out there," Suga said in October 2018, "but maybe we could perform at the Super Bowl some day." Now, that would be a sight to see!

"WE HAVE LEARNT TO LOVE OURSELVES, SO NOW I URGE YOU TO 'SPEAK YOURSELF'," HE SAID. "NO MATTER WHO YOU ARE, WHERE YOU'RE FROM, YOUR SKIN COLOUR, GENDER IDENTITY: SPEAK YOURSELF." RM, AT THE UN

TOP BTS perform in Paris to celebrate the official visit of the South Korean president, October 14, 2018.

ABOVE The ARMY show their love at a 'Love Yourself' concert, September 9, 2018

59

Looking relaxed after their ground-breaking *Good Morning America* appearance, September 26, 2018.

GENERATION UNLIMITED

Before news of the band's debut movie broke the internet in October 2018, BTS returned to the stage in a much more poignant manner during the previous month, when the group became the first Korean boy band to address the United Nations (UN) General Assembly. Their appearance was designed to promote their Generation Unlimited initiative, which aims to ensure that every young person is in education, learning, training or employment by 2030 – a cause that is very close to BTS's hearts. As the band's popularity and influence have grown since 2013, they have also increased their passion for promoting the value of believing in yourself. BTS give young adults a platform upon which to discuss their struggles with self-worth, self-doubt and mental health. Dressed in dark suits – rather different from their usual outfits! – RM led the band in speaking to the UN, delivering a speech that deeply moved fans and critics alike. "In an intro to one of our early albums, there is a line that says, 'My heart stopped when I was maybe 9 or 10.' Looking back, I think that's when I began to worry about what other people thought of me and started seeing myself through their eyes," RM said. "I stopped looking up at the night sky, the stars. I stopped daydreaming. Instead, I tried to jam myself into the other moulds that other people made. Soon, I began to shut out my own voice and started to listen to the voices of others. No one called out my name and neither did I. My heart stopped, and my eyes closed shut. So, like this, I – we – all lost our names. We became like ghosts. There

was a small voice inside of me that said, 'Wake up, man, and listen to yourself.' But it took me quite a long time to hear music calling my real name. Even after making the decision to join BTS, there were a lot of hurdles. Some people might not believe it, but most people thought we were hopeless, and sometimes I just wanted to quit. I was very lucky that I didn't give it all up." Wise words, indeed. Check out genunlimited.org for more information or to get involved.

ABOVE The band receive some well-deserved recognition at the 2018 Korean Popular Culture and Arts Awards, Olympic Hall, Seoul, October 24, 2018.

RIGHT Dressed to impressed in matching suits for a performance fit for a president, October 14, 2018.

K-POPOGRAPHY

To new members of BTS's ARMY, the group's back catalogue of albums, EPs, singles, tours and TV shows can seem incredibly complex. The band, rather uniquely, release music in trilogies or series based on themes and concepts. This K-Popography of the band's releases hopefully will help you keep your collection up to date...

KOREAN ALBUMS
2 Cool 4 Skool (12 June 2013)
Dark & Wild (19 August 2014)
Wings (10 October 2016)
Love Yourself: Tear (18 May 2018)

JAPANESE ALBUMS
(Re-packaged Korean albums, in Japanese, with additional songs)
Wake Up (24 December 2014)
Youth (7 September 2016)
Mic Drop/DNA/Crystal Snow (6 December 2017)
Face Yourself (4 April 2018)

EPS
O!RUL8,2? (11 September 2013)
Skool Luv Affair (12 February 2014)
The Most Beautiful Moment in Life, Part 1 (29 April 2015)
The Most Beautiful Moment in Life, Part 2 (30 November 2015)
Love Yourself: Her (18 September 2017)

REISSUE ALBUMS
Skool Luv Affair Special Addition (14 May 2014)
You'll Never Walk Alone (13 February 2017)

TOURS
2014 BTS Live Trilogy Episode II: *The Red Bullet*
2015 BTS 1st Japan Tour *Wake Up: Open Your Eyes*
2015 BTS Live Trilogy Episode II: *The Red Bullet Tour*
2015 BTS LIVE *The Most Beautiful Moment in Life On Stage*
2016 BTS LIVE *The Most Beautiful Moment in Life On Stage: Epilogue*
2017 BTS Live Trilogy Episode III: *The Wings Tour*
2018 BTS World Tour: *Love Yourself*

Back to the start: BTS as they were on the edge of worldwide success! Can you guess the performance?